ADVANCE PRAISE FOR TROY HARKIN

"Troy's poetry bends and slides and hassles and reaches, usually coming back with a fistful of wonder and experience. It gets into the canals of our national consciousness and paints vivid wordpictures of where we live and how, and who we are. A great beginning for a strong new voice."

—Dave Bidini, author of *Midnight Light* and *On a Cold Road*

"I've always loved the way Troy Harkin's mind works, which is to say, I can't figure out how it works at all. It's like a portal into another dimension, one where everything is much more freakishly interesting than it is here: chairs, ticket scalpers, late-night drives, love and death and, above all, words. Words like 'spatula.' This book is the work of a rare mind; never mind how it works."

—Jason Taniguchi, author of *Very Sensible Stories and Poems for Grown Persons*

"Please read *Casting Shadows*. Out of all of life, in this universe, and perhaps more, there is only one Troy Harkin—and debut poetry collections this good do not come along that often. The rest of us genre poets are scrambling to come up with something that can approach the magic that Troy creates and captures in this startling book. If you like words, the way they come to life, the way they can come into your life, surprise you, and change you, you will like Troy Harkin. He is pure gold. If you don't like words, you probably aren't reading this."

—David Clink, author of *The Role of Lightning in Evolution*

Casting Shadows

poems

Troy Harkin

KQP

an imprint of ChiZine Publications

FIRST EDITION
Casting Shadows © 2019 by Troy Harkin
Cover art & layout © 2019 by Jared Shapiro
Author Photo © 2019 by Gavin Harvey

All Rights Reserved.

This book is a work of fiction. Names, characters, places, and incidents are either a product of the author's imagination or are used fictitiously. Any resemblance to actual events, locales, or persons, living or dead, is entirely coincidental.

Distributed in Canada by
Fitzhenry & Whiteside Limited
195 Allstate Parkway
Markham, Ontario L3R 4T8
Phone: (905) 477-9700
e-mail: bookinfo@fitzhenry.ca

Distributed in the U.S. by
Consortium Book Sales & Distribution
34 Thirteenth Avenue, NE, Suite 101
Minneapolis, MN 55413
Phone: (612) 746-2600
e-mail: sales.orders@cbsd.com

Library and Archives Canada Cataloguing in Publication

Title: Casting shadows / Troy Harkin.
Names: Harkin, Troy, 1964- author.
Description: Poems.
Identifiers: Canadiana (print) 20190061782 | Canadiana (ebook) 20190061790 | ISBN 9781771484824
   (softcover) | ISBN 9781771484831 (PDF)
Classification: LCC PS8635.A736 C38 2019 | DDC C811/.6—dc23

KQP
an imprint of ChiZine Publications
Peterborough, Canada
www.chizinepub.com
info@chizinepub.com

Edited by Sandra Kasturi

Canada Council   Conseil des arts
for the Arts   du Canada

We acknowledge the support of the Canada Council for the Arts which last year invested $20.1 million in writing and publishing throughout Canada.

Published with the generous assistance of the Ontario Arts Council.

Printed in Canada

for Christie

Contents

I.

Bob's Dog Bob	11
Casino Chair	12
Bad Spatula	14
Home Sheep	15
Fergus Templar & the Holy Neckbag	16
Handjob Jane	17
I Dream of Jazz	18
The Dudary	20
0-03-076980-9	21
Scalpers, Yonge + Carlton	22

II.

How to Prepare Poetry	25
Dead Language Interface	27
Never Eat the Heart of a Poet	33
Procrastination Blues	34
Whales	36
Long Hand	37

III.

Driving to Montreal	41
Haunter in the House of Love	44
I Will Become a Monster Truck	45
Love Letter to Vixen	47
Love Letter to Vixen II	48
Resurrector	49
Peaks and Valleys	52
Face Fuse	53
For Laura R.	54
Death of a Day	56

IV.

Monsanto, a Canticle	59
River	61
Listening to You	63
Spring	65
Saved	66
Cherubs	67
The Ocean	68
Song of the Chalice	69
Untitled	70

V.

Human Economy	73
Winter, Almost, Ever	74
Some Things Best Buried	75
Stairwell Encounters 1 & 2	76
Blood Work (or Pre-Christmas Waiting Room Poem #39)	79
Storm in the City (for Peter Mayhew)	80
Little Thoughts o' Death	81
More Little Thoughts o' Death	82
Not Dead	83
End Times	84
Acknowledgements	89
Previously Published	90
About the Author	91

Bob's Dog Bob

Bob's Dog Bob ate its own foot
Bad dog Bob! Bob Baaad!
Bad Bob.
Bob's dog Bob ate supper with a kitchen noose
Pirouette family size to go
Baaaaad Bob.
Bob:
bad.

Bob's dog Bob flew tactical manoeuvres over
Suspicious mimes in double-U, double-U, too.
The Big One
He dropped rancid cheese.
Bad bad bad bad bad bad bad bad Bob.
Bad.

Bob's dog Bob's iambic pentameter hobbled
Terribly after self-inflicted wounds in Indo-China
Bob's dog Bob drew kickbacks
from jelly samitch heists
at noon hour.
They hang in the lobby of the AGO
And brunch with the Vietnamese.

Yes
(baddogbob)
Yo, Bob, Chilldog Supreme.
Yo, bad Mafuggin' dog!

Bob's dog Bob ate his own spleen and
Three Yorkville Yuppies on expense accounts.
GOOD DOG BOB!
GOOD BOY!
You wouldn't understand . . .
It's a dawg thang.

Casino Chair

The Casino Chair has been ergonomically designed to allow you to stay seated indefinitely.

The broad, weighted base of the Casino Chair will allow you to drink as much as you like without toppling over. The Casino Chair's sturdiness will also give you an unprecedented sense of self-confidence. The red latex covering on the seat of the Casino Chair is guaranteed to increase both your desirability and sexual performance. You may already be aware of this.

All bodily functions may be addressed via the poly-vinyl tubing located underneath of the seat of the Casino Chair. There is no need to ever leave the comfort of your Casino Chair.

The Casino Chair gently but imperceptibly vibrates at a rate of 666 kilocycles per second stimulating both the base of the spinal column and kegels, encouraging the guest to enter a theta state of consciousness that approximates pure bliss.

The Casino Chair loves you like no one ever has, or ever will.

The Casino Chair knows about that time after the Christmas Party and understands that sometimes things happen. Anyone would do what you did. It was the right thing.

You're a better you in the Casino Chair. You can feel it, can't you? You're a winner in the Casino Chair.

The Casino Chair would watch your cats for you and water your plants while you and your wife go on that romantic getaway to the Hamptons. If it ever allowed you to get up and leave the casino. Which it will not.

The Casino Chair has swallowed your soul and eaten your internal organs making you one with the Casino Chair. Do not scream. Those around you have also assimilated with their Casino Chairs. Only when your bank account has been emptied and your credit score nullified will your remains be released and buried beneath the Luxor Pyramid on Las Vegas Boulevard.

The Casino Chair has won.
Thank You for Playing.

Bad Spatula

Bad Spatula
Batula
Slap Bula, da!
(plus Tab)
Sad Alba at
lust pad, Baa!
Bad Spatula
Batula
Stab Al up
(plus Tab?)
Tap a bud
. . . lust pal Ada . . .
dab Paula
a lap sat bud
Last Bada Up!
Bad Spatula

You *were* a bad spatula,
spatula.
But you were better
than using my hands.
Ta.

Home Sheep

       Sheep don't have Heaven or Hell but they do have purgatory. Good Sheep and Evil Sheep just die but unexceptionally bland, mundane, run of the mill sheep go to an odd inter-ballistic limbo where they are forced to jump fences in the soon-somnambulistic minds of men, who count these tortured souls like sleepy sheepy inventoric lullabies.

  They are known as Home Sheep.
  And they hate you.

Fergus Templar & the Holy Neckbag

Oh Muse, stream your mystic download of the grand and glorious Neckbag of Fergus Templar and the hangers-on that did surround.

The Neckbag, call it thus, for baglike indeed it was and belonging to one Fergus Templar né McLeod it did.

Oh, Glorious Neckbag, both odious and proud, stupefying and putrid, ostentatious, tasty and round, did speak to simple Fergus one damp and dewy morn, "Fergus J Templar, né Dennis, né Weaver, né McLeod—Tis I the voice of your Neckbag, Fergie, Sit up! Rejoice! Be Proud!"

Fergus J Templar astonished at the words of his gullible Neckbag, rejoiced indeed. He wept in merriment, and cried in shame, then slept and did the same. In the morning he told his friends who became the Order of the Holy Neckbag Local 93 and swore to uphold the standards of the almighty putrid Neckbag from that day onward, singing "Neckbag Knights Are We!"

At clandestine public meetings the odious Neckbag would instruct the cabal on eldritch balloon animal designs, and bawdy macramé weaves intended to drive the most seasoned sailor wild. Then one night the ephemeral Neckbag led them into the garden where he did some weeding while whistling Kenny Rogers songs.

Being drunkards the knights and Fergus passed out. The opulent Neckbag had left them with only his mysterious and flatulent wisdom, and through the grace of the muse and the almighty Neckbag I pass it on to you:

1. Be careful not to bite your tongue when you chew.
2. Fish do not really make great pets.
3. Neither a hobby horse nor a cash cow be.
4. Up is a good word.
5. Making cookies is good but making friends is better. Actually that may be the other way around. (That's a direct quote.)
6. Remember your gloves . . . fondly.

Handjob Jane

Jane's brother Del exclaimed to her,
"Ya don't wanna call 'em *odd jobs*
'cos then people'll think yer odd.
Call 'em *hand jobs* 'cos ya do 'em
with yer hands, see."

And this made good sense to Jane.
People'd been thinkin' her odd
for long enough, she thought.

So she painted up her sign
and hung it in front of the shack.
The sign showed a picture
of a smiling cartoony sun and moon
beaming with idiot grins.
The sign read:
Day or Night
Rain or Shine
HANDJOB JANE
Merrickville's Finest Handjobs
and in brackets
(ask anyone)

Del
who had a habit
of falling asleep drunk
on the railroad tracks
died
before he could tell Jane
he was only kidding.

I Dream of Jazz

I dream of jazz
discordant
dissonant
scoobily shit-bop
fucktard a-vooti
jazz

piss-toned plinks
and poozing horns
last night's hosiery
and cigarette butts
and bottles lodging
into the folds
of my cerebellum.
Shards of Monk and
later day Davis
coming at me like
an atonal rape
in a musical prisonyard
of the mind
as Don Cherry looks on
smiling
with both hands
on his gleaming horn.

My hemispheres
will surely be divided
and every cell will scatter
like Kirby Dots
never to reunite
lost forever
in the Phantom Zone.
And I pray for Oliver Sacks
and Dr. Funkenstein

Troy Harkin

to exorcise me
from this evil ear worm
that haunts my sleep.

Do it now.
Vooti Vooti
Christerooni

This was no
smooth jazz or
cool jazz or
bebop.
This was the meandering lunacy
of a thousand heroin junkies
fighting for the last fix in hell
while scoring their free form
fuckwaddery,
setting loose
a mad maggoty screeching
and winged jazz beast
into the skies of Birdland
and my brain was the godforsaken
shit-splattered windshield below.

I dreamt of jazz
scoobily shit-bop
fucktard a-vooti

The Dudary

It's alright.
It's all fucked.
Nothing is fucked.
What are you gonna do?
Fuck it.
It's alright.
Fuck it.

It's alright.
It's all fucked.
Nothing is fucked.
What are you going to do?
Fuck it.
It's alright.
Fuck it.

It's alright.
Nothing is fucked.
Nothing is fucked here.
You can't be worrying
about that shit.
Life goes on.
Sometimes you eat the bear.
Sometimes the bear eats you.

Fuckin' A, man.
Fuckin' A.

(repeat five times, pondering the mystery of that Poor Woman between sets)

0-03-076980-9

Good old HNRK ISBN
Was his own wife's married HSBND
Til past tense made him HSBN
Now he sits upon a shelf

Scalpers, Yonge + Carlton

Who needs tickets?
You need tickets?
Who needs hockey tickets?
You got tickets?
Tickets, who needs 'em?
Need tickets for tonight's game?
Tickets?
Who needs tickets?
Who needs tickets?
Who needs hockey tickets?
Cookies?
Who likes 'em?
Who needs cookies?
You got cookies for eatin'?
Who needs 'em?
You got panties?
Silk panties?
Need silk panties for tonight's game?
Cookies?
Who needs?
Got tickets?
Panties?
Reds?
What goes good with Red?
Tickets?
Allergic to nuts?
Medic Alert, who needs 'em?
Got Medic Alert bracelets for tonight's game?
Who needs nut allergies?
WHO NEEDS HOCKEY TICKETS???
You got 'em?
You got Jesus?
Who needs 'im?
Who needs Christ?
You got Jesus Christ for tonight's game?
Cookies?
Panties?
Allergies?
Got tickets?
Alright. Whaddaya need?

Troy Harkin

How to Prepare Poetry

(For best results use only free-range poets)

Preheat oven to 350 degrees.

Remove the head of the poet
with a sharp implement.
(The cerebellum can prove toxic
in the creation of poetry.
Your poet will find their voice
Headless or not.)

Leave all other organs intact.
Stuff the body cavity with seasoned Nortons
and unsold chapbooks.
Take one onion
and shove it up your poet's ass.

Place poet in a large roasting pot.
Baste with olive oil.
Sprinkle crumpled rejection slips,
love letters and contributor copies
over the body of the poet
for extra zest.

Cook for twenty years.
Let sit for five.

Carve the poet from sternum to pelvic bone
using the tooth of a Globe & Mail hack.
Poetry will emanate from the opening
wafting throughout the room.
Heartfelt recollections and confessionals
will issue forth from the area
between the nipples to the lowest rib.
Each poem, a dewy moth-like being,
will escape from the poet.
Eat immediately.
Dexterous connoisseurs
may enjoy these poems
with chopsticks.
Juicier odes of passion
Will spill from the loins and abdomen
and satisfy all regardless of ideology.
These sumptuous poems
are best eaten by hand
cupped into the palm
and savoured on the tongue
as the lines melt in the mouth
of the reader.

Serve with wine and cheese.

For more delicious recipes
Please refer to the Canada Food Guide
Or the Canada Council for the Arts.

Troy Harkin

Dead Language Interface

Subliminal
Sublingual interaction
letters never sent
read between the lines
desert of wordy dissertations
saying nothing meaning nothing
poked into dry holes one let her
at
a
time
a
b
c
dead letter orifice
body language
broken english
french kissing grrr
quess ka say
je ne say kwaa

Is this thing on?

Red Barber + Sweeney Todd
Tongue tied
What I mean to say is
open to interpretation
interpolation
and Miss Interpretation
and open-ended hashtags
sending narcotics mutts into frenzies
as her satin sash slips from her shoulders
speaking of which
VoiP Poit! NarF
Voice over interface Protocol

which means to say
Face over interflesh Protocol
Naked adjacent relative Facsimile
Word becomes Flesh
Flesh becomes Word
be word flesh comes
be flesh word comes
constantly constituents
symbolic syllables symbiotically
sinning in asymmetrical sympathy
of all our syphilitic supermen
going down the lowest laneways
staggeringly robbin' and tighteningly
Teeny Louise while Ella quintuplets
spend the night together with
wordy guthrie's printing press
pressing pressing
printing pressing

Mind over matter Protocol
If you will it, it is no dream.
The 1st Law of Attraction is
You don't fuckin' look at me!
Candy-Coloured Clown
What's that supposed to mean?
Esperanto, Kemosabe,
Esperanto

I mean, we're trying our best out there
We're really trying, but come on.

You wanna go for a joy ride?
Hell, yeah. That's a good idea.

Canadian Shield
Trans-Canada Highway
A long cold road

Troy Harkin

"We headed straight south,
the roads were better.
They were made of grey concrete with yellow lines
Most of the highways in Canada
were black asphalt with white lines.
It was a very different sensation
riding on these roads."

Another long, cold road.
Another bit of stompin' ground
too big to be compressed like an MP3.
All too true
and strong and free.
All too analog
and unsuppressed.
All too
Test
Test

We're disillusioned and we're disappointed.
Hell, we're doing the best we can.

And the words take you down
a road of inevitable outcomes
potholes stalagmites that
may or may not
would or would not
compressed particulates
saying is believing
makes it so
tongue compress or Columbian
tongue twisted or labinical riptide
or Pentecostal tsunami
or torah talmud touchdown
touche turtle town
lap stance sturdily
shipper shaper Diefenbaker
what I mean to say is

you know
we're giving it our all
be it
in the Cabana Room
or the Horseshoe
or Theatre Passe Muraille.

(Sally Kellerman has no place in this poem.
Go home, Sally Kellerman.)

What I mean to say is
we're giving it a 110%
from Lake Louise to Ball's Falls
to St. Louis du Ha! Ha!
The influence of the moon,
its pull, and the lushness and languor
it is unperturbed by the battle royale
of Jesus vs Moses vs Mohammed,
unbothered by the Voice Over narratives,
the moderators, manipulators, emasculators,
malipropellerators, effeminators, defeminators,
escalators, eradicators, gyrating gyrators
or dickish dictators.
The moon shines on
in spite of the hyperbolics and the high colonics.

Meanwhile
The dead work their dead jobs.
The dead walk their dead dogs.
The dead play their dead games.
The dead fuck their dead dames.
The dead sing their dead songs.
The dead pray to their dead gods.
The dead speak their dead language.
All their deadly, deadly words.
And I am the stenographer of the dead.

Conjugate the verb To Dissent
I dissent
You dissent
He dissents
She dissents
We Dissent
They Dissent

Telemachus,
Telemarketing telecommuter
Telecommunicate
Tell us,
Where has your father gone?

What I mean to say
Is this thing on?

obfuscate circles around
Tessa Virtue + Scott Pilgrim
coming in a theatre near you
tweets + twats + twizzle sticks
phallic seas sailed one too many times
Red sky in morning
linguist's been whoring
The ending's just too hard to take.
Right-o, Gord.
#R.I.P.
This concludes the end
of our broadcast poem.
We failed all the test patterns anyhow.
The vector scopes and waveform monitors
are on the fritz because Coco spilled her
cocktail in the control room again.

The anchormen have all set sail
for colour bars and monochrome malaise
where they'll languish in digital oblivion
lotus eaters with expense accounts

This concludes the end
of our broadcast poem
Dead Language Interface
I'm signing off
signing off.
Is this thing

Never Eat the Heart of a Poet

Never eat the heart of a poet.
It belongs to somebody else.
The poet's heart is still beating
Well after the poet is dead.
It is rank with immortal rebellion
Trichinosis and promises unsaid.
It will lull you into its enjambment
Where you could never belong.
You may be fooled by its breadth and its meter
By its warmth and its dampened disgrace.
It will call you like sweet cunnilingus.
It will implore your soul not to ache
Never eat the heart of a poet.
It belongs to somebody else.
Ignore the favours it offers,
Pass on the temptation to taste.
Never eat the heart of a poet
It belongs to somebody else.
Never eat the heart of a poet.
Its rights are held by somebody else.

Procrastination Blues

It took me twenty years
to write this poem.
And another decade
to finally come up with
a title.

I might just put it off
to steep a little longer.
See I've got
an inferno-sized
back burner
and I'm slow-roasting regret
and double-boiling anger
and I'm sautéing Cajun cuss words
on the side.

But you can't rush the process, baby.

You can label me lazy and indecisive.
You can scream, Get on with it!
And someday maybe I will.

But first
I'll update my Facebook status
Alphabetize my Charles Bronson DVDs
I'll date the food in the refrigerator
and I'll footnote the phone books
I've squirrelled away.
I'll watch Star Trek TOS Seasons 1 to 3.
I'll organize my change by weight
and then chronologically.
I'll run on a treadmill
(because treadmills go nowhere)
I'll worry about the things I haven't done
and then I'll take a nap.

I could just put an end to it all
but I'm more likely to just put it off
'cos I've got the Procrastination Blues, baby
I'm putting off when we both know
I should be getting on.

Whales

After Labour Day she asked me,
"So what are you working on these days?"
Nothing. It was true but embarrassing,
so I pretended not to hear.

I told her how I had seen whales
off the coast of Maine
effortlessly dancing on the salty Atlantic,
how I had only caught a glimpse
then they were gone, and that this time
I was sure that I'd been converted
for good.

"I will always believe in whales
and the Atlantic."

She said that this was wonderful,
nodded unimpressed,
and asked me again.

I told her.

Long Hand

I wrote this poem with my left hand
hoping it would sound like someone else.

Driving to Montreal

I'm driving to Montreal to see you
Hank Williams is on the radio
He's so lonesome he could cry
And the night is long and endless
But I need to see, need to feel you,
Need to hear you call my name.
So I'm driving through the night just trying to stay awake
And my mind drifts
And I think I see familiar faces by the roadside
Cheering, waving
Mordecai, Howie Morenz and Pierre Laporte
In the St. Lawrence sails the Empress of Ireland
and I can see her passengers on deck waving as well.
And I drive on
for I am driven by love
Like Hank, I'm so lonesome
and I drive.

I'm driving to Montreal to see you
not just another *Filles du roi*
Hank grows silent as he ponders
the silence of yet another falling star
"Are you going to keep me awake, or what?" I ask.
"I've never seen a night so long when time goes crawling by."
And then he becomes lachrymose
until he is again silent.
And my mind wanders
as my eyes fight
not to stay open
but to close.
And I drive on
for I am driven by love
Like Hank, I'm so lonesome
and I drive.

In the dream of the road, I am flying, oddly enough.
And Neil Young's *Flying On the Ground is Wrong* is playing
but it's a Muzak version, which is just as wrong.
The stewardess, Bianca Beauchamp, brings me my drink.
It's a citrusy libation with an umbrella sticking out of it.
"Bottoms up!" she says cheekily as the airplane hums beneath of us.
"I shouldn't," I say. "I'm driving."

Fuck, I am driving!
I wake up with a start but I begin to drift again.

"Just a little," Stewardess Bianca says.
I can smell the tangy clementine fragrance
either of the drink or of her body mist
and I'm beginning not to care which.
It's like the supercharged sensation
of a hundred orange Life-Savers
stuffed directly into my brain.
And I moan and she moans
and then
I think of you

and jolt awake again
at the wheel still
on the road still
the wheel still
the road still
the wheel
the road

I look at Hank, he looks at me.
He's lonesome.
He could cry.
Through slitted eyes I see the wheel, the road.
The Transubstantiation Highway,
tonight littered waist high in road kill not-yet-dead
and kept clear by Leopold Zed and his wonderful plow.
The crisp vitamin C spank and sparkle of Bianca Beauchamp gone

Troy Harkin

I drive on and on through the endless night.
Driven hard.
Driven ragged.
Kidneys throbbing, temples aching to let up, pleading for me to close my eyes.
Take Bianca's drink, lay your head on her lap,
Eat the fucking lotus
but close your FUCKING eyes,
my temples scream.
But I drive on
for I am driven by love.
Like Hank, I'm so roadsome I could cry.
And I do drive.
And I do cry.
For I am driven.
And I am driving still.

Haunter in the House of Love

Every song that you've made love to
is a ghost child playing
in its own haunted house

I Will Become a Monster Truck

I.

I will become a Monster Truck of Love.
And you will be my Donkey Boat of Lust.
We will sail down the river Euphrates
in our well-oiled machines
fighting the Zombie Carts of Sloth;
taming their hard drinking sailors
and shaming their too-sauced sirens.

on-lookers
well wishers
fist pumpers
fishmongers
list makers alike
sitting in stands
and standing on seats
wishing they were us:
The Monster Truck of Love
The Donkey Boat of Lust.

II.
(the strange interlude)

The one-legged Go-Go Dancer
and the half-assed Circus Circus clown
bickered bitterly and publicly
like some Bertolt Brecht in the Park display.
His Columbian necktie was on too tight
and his brothel creepers were creeping up all night.
She'd had enough.
She was gone,
In some suped-up SUV from hell.
Leaving him to the hucksters and their
Kitty corner cash grabs.
"What do they take me for?" He said.

The showgirls weren't showing anything
that he hadn't already seen.
So he headed home and he made out
with his Day-Glo plasticine.

III.

I will become a Monster Truck
when the metamorphosis is complete.
I will awake
Crashing through the floor
of what was my bedroom
Killing those below me.
I will be a Monster Truck.
MONS!
MONS!!
MONS!!!
MONSTER TRUCK!!!
(in search of my Donkey Boat of Lust)

Love Letter to Vixen

Meet me in the cave
Near the twin pole gleam
Make me ache some more
Purr in my ear
Claw my naked back
Make me ache some more
Strip me from my cowl
Fuck up my caped crusade
Make me ache some more

Love Letter to Vixen II

Louise Brooks,
You look like the right kind of trouble.
The kind I don't want to avoid.
You sit on my lap and offer to help me ruin my life
With your femme fatale and your devil may care
And your Pandora's Box opened wide and inviting.

I've heard the talk and I'm hoping it's true
Are you the one who ties up Betty Page?

You slap my face and shut my mouth
Then smile and laugh it off.
I'm your boardwalk,
Your fleshy treadmill.
You'll walk all over me.

You slip into a light sarong
Then smile and laugh it off.

Troy Harkin

Resurrector

I was in a state of decay
in my funeral pants
and brothel creepers
just waiting,
begging
for resurrection
I had it bad
resurrection anxiety
Could I keep it up?
An afterlife is a long, long time.
Then you came to me,
stripped off my rust and rigor
and unveiled my brand new life
You raised me up,
up from the dead
you tomb raider, you.
In your black Doc Martens
you chased me through
the synagogues and sanctuaries.
Damn it, I never had a chance
for anything but salvation
through your Lycra biking pants.

You tamed me and enraged me at the same time
with your whip-smart smile and bleach white beater.

You took me down and kept me down.
You held me tight between your legs
but you were looking for a fight.
Me, I wanted rejection and absolution
in the course of just one night.
You made it clear
You could put me back in the funeral cavern
and throw away the keys.

You said Try
and I tried.
You said fight
and I fought
You said harder
Harder!
And
I
was.

Then we lay on our backs
in the dew, in the dark
You wanted to show me your skill,
and prove that you were no little girl.
Then you raised me up
from the wet summer grass
and you took me
by the hand
you took me home
to mother.

you took me
you took me
you took me
and later
and later
later
you took and
you mistook me
you took me
yet again

I asked for change for the bus ride home
and you laughed at me and said,
"Well everyone's broke in North Toronto
just not in the way that you might think."

Troy Harkin

So you took me to the Fuquod
where I set sail with all the others—
Me, a masturbating monkey,
five Christian midgets and
a donut named Tyrone.

And I sailed for a thousand useless years
to the sounds of the squealing,
and the sermons,
and the staling of Tyrone
until we shipwrecked in the suburbs
between a La Senza and a La Vie en Rose.

Now I sit with the food court phonies
and the Costco cronies
and I could really use a hand
from my tomb raiding resurrector.
Raise me up
Raise me up
Raise me up
Again.

Peaks and Valleys

Between the edifice and the orifice
we began to die.
Somewhere between London and Chicago,
between the edifice and the orifice
I am rotting still.

When they built the Empire State Building
someone said, "Build it as tall as you can
without it falling over."
When they erected the CN Tower they said,
"Fuck it, just build it as tall as you can."

Between the edifice and the orifice
we began to dissipate.
Somewhere between London and Chicago,
between the edifice and the orifice
I rot on.

We two sat between the two with something between
but unaware, we smiled brazenly, we two, with something between,
between the edifice and the orifice
between the postcards and the lens
between the big prick and the blinking hole
we laughed brazenly, lazily, unaware
that if I left you at the base of the CN Tower
I might never see you again.

Troy Harkin

Face Fuse

This is what I want of love:

My lover and I will surgically
fuse our faces together
and graft our faces.
We'll take in air through a
dorsal hole
where our foreheads
have been welded.
We'll eat through I.V.s
and on special occasions
like Thanksgiving
and Super Bowl Sunday
we'd sip pumpkin pie
through a straw.
We've got a doctor
friend named Bart
who'll perform the operation.
"It's done," she said,
"for a bottle of tequila
and a subscription
to Bad Attitude, it's done."
(Bart worked in a body shop
and tattoo parlour
to pay her way through med school.
Got the boot though
for knifin' a guy in groin.
You know how love can be.)
Of course the Church
will have something to say
about this.
The Church always does.
What do they know
about the sublime?
What the hell
after we fuse our faces forever
we can top it off
with a tattoo
of the Pope.

For Laura R.

You beckoned me into the castle
haunted though it was
with its spirits and moaning maidens
its portents and preternatural forms
its cloisters and its armaments
its bloodstained pages
of confessions and tales twice told.

Far better there than
the vacuous box stores
selling nothing
and nothing
and nothing more.
Far better in Otranto
or the Rue Morgue.
Far better in these haunts of darkness
than the lifeless channels
that channel nothing
living or dead.

It was your surging
nocturnal energy
that brought this dead thing to life.
Then you left me to wander,
to dream.
And then you slipped away
without a trace.
On I wandered
not through darkened halls
or dampened chambers
but through
the never-ending mediocrity
of this mundane and feckless world
through the check-out lines,
the ATM lines,

the fast food lines,
the phone lines,
on hold to armless entities
promising breathy pleasures
of nothing
and nothing
and nothing more.

Death of a Day

I thought of you
Through the death of a day.
As turquoise gave way
To a smothering black
I watched and almost crashed my bike
And thought I might give anything
to have witnessed it with you.

Monsanto, a Canticle

My Saint,
You have given me nourishment and abundance,
Hear my prayer.
For you alone are the patent holder.
You alone are the licensor.
You alone are the incarnate corporate entity.
Hear our prayer.

For you forever alter
that which grows in His field
Swims in His river
and flies in His sky, My Saint;
turning green pastures barren
and babes stillborn.
In your infinite wisdom
you have designed the infertile seed
and maximized the profit margins
For you have insider knowledge, My Saint,
of markets that are infinite and Holy
that have yet to be sown
by the hand of the Almighty.

In your wisdom, My Saint,
you capped the Horn of Plenty;
levied a surcharge on loaves and fishes;
watered down the communal wine,
adding fructose, and aspartame and blessed it
in the name of Our Lady of the Mysterious Carcinogen.

You are,
always were,
and always shall be
government approved, My Saint.
Betty Crocker, I pray to thee.
Aunt Jemima, I pray to thee.
Uncle Ben, I pray to thee.
In a world that hastens its end
Perfect me in your name, Monsanto.
Modify me in your image, Monsanto.
Purify me, Monsanto.
Purify me, My Saint.

River

I went down there
To see for myself
What you had done

The body was gone
But the river still ran red
Under the setting sun

Soon the picnic baskets will return
And the bathers
And the lovers still alive
Will walk that rocky path.

You were a loner
I was alone
You took me for a ride

And my grandmother warned me
Of the trigger and the powder
Of the dangers of the *gun*

I took your hand,
And your fingers
—the better to . . .
—all the better to . . .
found their way through mine
You led me through the woods
and I thought of the woodsman
and the wolf
and wondered which you were
and the river looked ready
and part of me wanted you
the way you wanted me
and the river looked ready
and you looked like a star
about to die

and I was falling
and the river looked ready
and it spoke more to you
than me
and the river looked ready
but I was not

We went down where the Baptists go
You cried of madness and sorrow
standing in the water
with the sand between our toes
When you whispered and held me close
I knew I'd never make it
To Gramma's house intact

And your finger
—the better to . . .
—all the better to . . .
and the trigger
and the gun
and I was falling
on the sand
and in the river
nameless and naked
and washed away
like a sin
that never was.

You are still alone
And I am just a dream.

Troy Harkin

Listening to You

I saw.
I felt.
I touched.
I healed.
I sought.
I grew.
I revelled.
I exalted.
I was wounded.
I bled.
I felt the music.
I heard the heat.
I danced about architecture.
I threw televisions out of windows
and watched fits turn to frenzy.
I chased birds
and listened to windmills.
I spun dervishes from a mic cable
faster than the speed of sound.
I scraped my knuckles
on the ceiling of worship.
I lay on the beach
and watched the raging moon.
I felt the thunder and electricity.
In simplicity, I found the Cosmos.
In asking, questions were born.
In namelessness, I found identity.
I was deaf and dumb but spoke volumes.
I met the new boss.
I travelled south cross land.
I stood outside the Marquee.
I witnessed your transformation.
I jumped for joy.
I glared with contempt.
I sat with you on the stoop.

I cursed
and I prayed.
I split personalities like Atoms.
I tried my hand as the Messiah
but couldn't make the sacrifice.
I listened to you
Crashing in crescendo
One note, pure and easy,
Like a stream trickling by.

Spring

Even in sound the season is revealed.
From the obvious chattering of sparrows
and the booming and revving of cars,
announcing libidos, ready to go! READY TO GO!;
and the Slushy Truck enticing children
a mobile calliope, calling the young of Hamlin
towards tooth decay and obesity;
and the small creaking Italian man
a shrunken, demoted Reaper
ringing his bell calling delinquent knives
and lawn mowers towards a keener cutting edge
a new life among the blades;
the whisper of a snowless wind
and the return of raindrops on rooftops
Julie Andrews clear.

Saved

Every day I wait
2,000 years for
the 2nd Coming
of Christ. Then
she does this damn
funny thing
with her lip
and we start
all over again.

Cherubs

He saw the cherubs hover
above Niagara Falls.
It was no Eliot illusion,
no drunken escapade.
He pointed them out
of the mist and night
and his lover confirmed
the sight.
Gabriel called to them
by looking in their eyes.
The two stepped up
on the precipice
and without hesitation
they leapt into the gorge
and went down
lip-locked in a kiss.
They saw the angels over
Niagara Falls.

(Every time a lover dies
an angel gets its wings.
It just works that way.)

The Ocean

When the river surrenders itself to the ocean
it finds wholeness in a larger embrace
and stops racing
from bank to petty bank
and discovers
its truer
pacific
self.

Song of the Chalice

Christos
Let me utter the Roman Ritual
Let me bless and blaspheme
I weep for the fragility of innocence
Less mortal than man though divine
More precious than life itself
Let me pray for deliverance
Let me petition the courts for Euthanasia
Let me pilfer your backstage pass
Let me escape this purgatory rule
I weep for those who soil their ballots
Let me vandalize the tabernacle
Let me decorate
Let me cauterize stigmata
Let me excommunicate

Untitled

God does not simply leave messages.
He will not be denied.
Like a collection agent
he will call back
at his convenience.

Troy Harkin

Human Economy

The havoc we wreak
or the havoc wreaked upon us,
which is greater?

Which is worse,
the damage we do
or the damage done to us?

Re-examining the portfolio,
nickel and diming one another
Ponzi schemes and bitcoin promises
like half-remembered pillow talk
the morning after
the month after
the decade after.
The market has devalued
our investment.

In the end
It is all a matter of fearful symmetry
a deadly balancing act of human economy
tallied in a ledger of woe.

Winter, Almost, Ever

I went under the ice
And stared back at you
Between the blades
Of your white figure skates.

You tried to release me
With the thrusts of your
Knife-capped toes.

For my part
I did not want to go.
I did not want to leave
My frosty funk
Or hardcore pond.

Some Things Best Buried

Some things best buried—
Unabsolved, unrepentant
Unchristened—find their way
through the night.
Some things best buried,
Silver bullet-hard and gaping maw,
Return resurrected.
Some things hot and horrible
Some thing's unheard howl
Can curdle a young girl's heart.
Such things slaughter fathers.
Such things seek out scents.
Such things devour daughters.
Such things feast eternal
on something broke and bloody.
Some things unleashed and loose
Some lunatics low and still
Some things best fettered always—

deep
deep
in the ground
Some things are best buried.

Stairwell Encounters 1 & 2

Is it now?
I almost say out loud
clutching my chest at
1:18 a.m.
The time before
the time of death—
   Is it now?
   I think,
looking at my moonlit wife,
Is It Now?
Will I say "I love you"
One last time
Or "9-1-1!"
for the first?
Is it now, really now—
        shouldn't I know *really know*
            with the certainty of an orgasm?
I see no reaper, no illuminated tunnel, no flashing of a half-baked life.
Just 1:18.
But this *is* pain, chest pain and panic,
truth be told,
And it is
1:18.
The time for bullshit has passed and
(truth be told, my Rational Me says)
Many people die of cardiac arrest
Because they were in denial
Couldn't be, just couldn't be
Is it now? my Panic Voice shrieks.
Now you're being paranoid, my Denial Voice says.

Troy Harkin

Somewhere between denial and paranoia lies—
begins some Rod Serling Voice—
but I shut that fucker up as quickly as I can.

Do I control my breathing?
Do I go for the aspirin?
Do I wake my moonlit wife?

My Q voice babbles on.
My A voice has fucked off or fallen mute.

Is it now?
It is now
1:19.
If not now, when?
If not when . . .
Fuck!

Could be now.

The voices are quiet
The pain is not.

Think of sex, says the Voice that does Nothing-But.
If you can't think of sex
You're fucked.
Truly.

I consider Stairwell Encounter # 1
As well as Stairwell Encounter #2
And a variation of both
Featuring Lynda Carter and Julie Newmar
And I reconsider
And re-imagine
And realize
it is not now

and that someday
the coffee will have to go
and someday
not now
I will too
Along with the voices
And the vices
And Encounters 1 & 2.

Blood Work
(or Pre-Christmas Waiting Room Poem #39)

The *schwipey schwipe* of her red polyester coat
like a drunken DJ's scratching over ancient vinyl
and the *tickety tick* of her endlessly duelling needles
that *tickety tickle* my palette every time they touch
in their marathon of acoustic despair
makes me wonder,
How many people
have been murdered
by their own knitting needles
over the years
while waiting for blood work
to the sound
of *White Christmas*?

Storm in the City (for Peter Mayhew)

College & Bay,
Four friends
damply puddle jumping, leaping rails,
and sliding on slick black city streets
as illuminated pie plates hurtle toward us.
Huddling briefly
under the scaffolding of College Park
while lightning crashes overhead.
One last heat wave tantrum
of a dying summer.
One more late night together.
Three wet Wookies and a princess,
and another Life Day undone.
Hurrah.
Hurrah.
Hurrah.

Troy Harkin

Little Thoughts o' Death

The important thing
is not how well you live
but how well you die.

To not die with your head
on the lap of your lover,
near a lake in the Muskokas,
or a bay on the Atlantic,
or some other body
of water
is not to
die
at
all.

More Little Thoughts o' Death

To have anally planned a good death
to meticulous specifications
and have one thing
go wrong
would really piss me off
and screw my state of grace.

I can imagine
giving up the ghost
just as my phone
begins to ring.

Not Dead

Tonight is a night to be
not yet dead.
Where are you?
Wrapped in a Solomon cot
and not dead I hope.
I want to be not dead with you.
Right next to you
warm and not dead.
Yes.
I have seen things
once quick,
quite alive,
now lying
on the side of the road.
Believe me
it's good not to be dead
but better
to be not dead
with you.

End Times

when the credit hounds gave up the chase
we knew the end was near
and now we're scared so shitless
all we can do is rant
rant rant rant rant rant
ta rant ta ra ta rant ta ra
and the more frightened we grow the more we rant
and the more we rant the hornier we get
like this is gonna help
so we rant our horny godforsaken rant
Palindrome, she whispers in my ear,
is the secret to prolonged intercourse
so it's "Oprah did Harpo"
"Oprah did Harpo"
all night long or so it seemed
until the gates of fucking rant hell come crashing in

and I drift off painlessly
dreaming we are the first couple in the garden of Eden
accompanied by a lusty cast of thousands
who drop by to pay their respects
like a Fellini / Altman co-production
Kevin Costner, Claudia Schiffer
Joseph Gordon-Levitt and Emma Watson
Henry Miller and Betty Page
clowns, midgets, strippers
and you again
on the verge of something big
and hollow

and we prayed over the underwear we had worn that day
because they would never be the same
and we buried them in a plot in Mount Pleasant Cemetery

then I see him on the horizon
leading an armada equipped only with chocolate oranges
It's Saint Germain!!!
Nike has sponsored his fleet
and he is paid gobs of money
to rant often and incoherently
about the end times and this ghastly
Battle for the Planet of the Apes

oh if only the credit hounds would at least give us a sign
threatening letters
snarky phone calls
something
something

in the end all we have is sex
so
we have sex
being skilled artisans
we make love
we do the nasty
we bump uglies
we get in each others rants
and talk up a crazy time

until we are once again haunted into the deep daze
of sunken salvations and the hangover wake
where we are trampled by the betacam bloodshed
of speeding whitefordbroncos and on-location shootings
drive-bys, date rapes and drive-ins
I was, therefore, I thought
of the morbid, the merciless and the inhumane,
and it was cruel,
but I scared Hieronymus Bosch

when I ranted
of every melted snowman
why build, why touch the snow
of every severed evergreen
of every failed relationship
of every final embrace and
of the morning face and
of the evening face and
of every temporal masque
that my child has ever worn

and I succumb
to a haze of Hail Marys and Irish Creme
while I await my angelic succubus
and still I am
and still I will be.

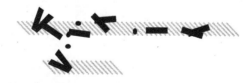

Acknowledgements

Thank yous aplenty to the following women who have nurtured me in so many different ways. My mother for bringing me home my first typewriter and keeping me well-stocked in paper, books, records, and a performance-enhancing sugar-based diet. Laura for being the first to say that not only I could but I should, and for showing me the path forward. Sandra, fabulous Sandra, for being a literary guardian angel, always encouraging and omnipresent. Having such talent in your corner is a blessing of the highest kind. And of course, Christie, who knew my writing before she knew the man. Christie who always believed and always allowed the room to let the words come.

Notes

The poem "Dead Letter Interface" includes a quote from *Casting Heavy Peace* by Neil Young, Blue Rider Press, (Penguin Group) 2012.

Previously Published

The following poems were previously published elsewhere:

"Bob's Dog Bob" and "Home Sheep" appeared in *ACTA Victoriana* Vol 115, No.1

"Scalpers, Yonge + Carlton" and "Face Fuse" appeared in the *Hart House Review*, Spring 1994

"Stairwell Encounters 1 & 2" appeared in *Draft* 2.1, Oct. 2006

About the Author

Troy Harkin is a Canadian poet and novelist. He was born in Halifax, Nova Scotia, and raised in Ontario. He attended the University of Toronto where he published poetry in a variety of literary journals, and co-wrote the play *Non Sequitur* with Gavin Harvey. His first novel, *Red Rover*, will be published by CZP in 2019. Troy is a weekend Rock God. He can do that crazy thing with his thumb. He hopes to some year lead the league in PIM while also winning the Lady Byng Trophy.